Original title:

The Palm Tree Pathway

Copyright © 2025 Creative Arts Management OÜ

All rights reserved.

Author: Riley Hawthorne

ISBN HARDBACK: 978-1-80581-564-8

ISBN PAPERBACK: 978-1-80581-091-9

ISBN EBOOK: 978-1-80581-564-8

Serenity Among Swaying Fronds

Beneath the fronds, a dance we start,
The breeze, it plays a cheeky part.
With rustling leaves that giggle loud,
We sway and twirl beneath the crowd.

Oh, how the shadows tease our feet,
As we attempt a tricky feat.
A spin, a trip, we almost fall,
But laughter rises, conquering all.

The Oasis of Memory Lane

In shade we reminisce and sigh,
With coconut dreams that drift on by.
Each tale is sweeter than the last,
Yet surely, some were far too fast.

A parrot squawking in the mix,
Chiming in with funny tricks.
We laugh until our bellies ache,
This paradise is ours to make.

Embrace of the Island Breeze

The breeze rolls in, a playful tease,
It tugs at hats with joyful ease.
Sunglasses slide; oh, what a sight!
Chasing them brings sheer delight.

We swing and sway, arms in the air,
Like humans caught in a dance affair.
With every gust, a new surprise,
Watch out for frisbees, they can fly!

Footprints on the Tropical Trail

Each step we take, a squishy sound,
Flip-flops slapping on the ground.
Crabs join in with their quick scuttle,
We laugh as they cause quite the cuddle.

The path ahead, a jungle gym,
With giggles loud and chances slim.
Some trip and tumble, land in sand,
But smiles emerge, it's all so grand.

Harmony in the Palm's Embrace

Beneath the palms, the squirrels dance,
Their tiny shorts, quite by chance.
One takes a leap, the crowd goes wild,
A sight that makes the sunbeam smiled.

Coconuts fall with a thunderous thud,
As seagulls squawk, who'd get the dud?
We giggle at the beach ball's plight,
Waves crash against, oh what a sight!

A parrot steals the beachcomber's hat,
And does a jig, imagine that!
Sunblock on noses, all turn red,
As laughter echoes from beach to bed.

With flip-flops flying in the breeze,
We chase the seagulls, do as you please.
The sun dips low, we wave goodbye,
To this grand scene beneath the sky.

Echoes of a Tropical Dream

The sunset paints the sky with cheer,
Frogs in sunglasses leap with beer.
They croak and ribbit like a band,
A concert on the golden sand.

Lemons rolling, giggling loud,
As friends all gather, quite a crowd.
Chasing limes that roll away,
What a funny game to play!

A crab in flip-flops seeks a mate,
With dance moves that can't hesitate.
He moonwalks sideways, proud and spry,
As everyone just laughs and sighs.

With coconuts upon our heads,
We prance and dance, forget our beds.
The tropical night is all aglow,
In dreamlike chaos, we all flow.

A Journey to Evergreen Bliss

On a curious path, we travel silly,
With vibrant birds that hop and frilly.
They wear sunglasses and dance around,
Each step we take feels joy profound.

Mice in hats share tales of old,
About the cheese that turned to gold.
They giggle, squeak, 'Oh what a bite!'
Under the stars, we dine in light.

Banana peels beneath our feet,
A slip, a tumble, oh what a feat!
We laugh until the stars all wink,
As fruits join in, and we all think.

The tree trunks twist in jolly ways,
They nod and sway, join in the plays.
With every laugh, the moonlight glows,
In evergreen bliss, our joy just grows.

The Colors of Tropical Solitude

In hues so bright, they dance and sway,
Bananas wear smiles, in a fruity display.
Coconuts giggle, as they drop with a thud,
While mangoes shout jokes, in a sweet, juicy flood.

A parrot in pajamas, oh what a sight,
Telling tall tales, from morning till night.
Lemonade rivers flow, with a fizzy cheer,
While lizards wear sunglasses, without any fear.

Footsteps in the Shade

In between sunbeams, we skip with glee,
Dancing like ducks or a bumblebee.
Grass tickles our toes, it's a silly delight,
As shadows start giggling, oh what a sight!

We leap over puddles, splashing with flair,
Chasing our shadows, with no ounce of care.
A toucan offers us snacks from his stash,
As our laughter erupts in a colorful splash.

Nature's Divine Canopy

Under the whispers of rustling leaves,
The squirrels play poker, in their secret eaves.
We share silly secrets with butterflies free,
As sunbeams burst forth with a wink, 'Look at me!'

Fronds wave hello, as breezes join in,
While ants run marathons, competing to win.
A frog croaks a jingle, a modern-day bard,
As we roll on the grass, giggling hard.

Prelude to Tropical Serenity

As the twilight chuckles, the crickets take stage,
With fireflies winking, like stars on a page.
The breeze plays a tune, on a leafy guitar,
While we witness the show from a comfy bazaar.

Our woes hit the shelf, as the night starts to glow,
With moonlight painting smiles on faces aglow.
A hammock embraces us, swaying in laughter,
In this merry moment, the fun's only after.

Sunkissed Realms of Leisure

In a land where sunbeams play,
Frying eggs on rocks all day.
Seagulls steal my sandwich right,
As I munch with all my might.

Flip-flops dancing, toes in sand,
Sunscreen slathered, feeling grand.
Ice cream drips, a sticky treat,
Melting fast in summer heat.

A Canopy of Dreams Untold

Under silk and leaf we lay,
Listening to the insects' play.
Squirrels chatter, wisecracks fly,
A tree's joke? You won't believe your eye!

Coconut jokes from up so high,
Bouncing laughs like clouds on high.
The fruit falls down with quite a thud,
Reminding us to dodge the bud!

The Melody of Distant Waves

Waves are singing, a cheeky tune,
While I dance, under a cartoon moon.
My towel's flown, oh what a sight,
Caught by kids holding on so tight!

Seashells whisper tales of yore,
Opening jokes I've not heard before.
A crab pinches my toes, then scurries,
Leaving me in a fit of flurries!

Serendipity in the Shade

Life's a picnic, or so it seems,
Tangled in my ketchup dreams.
Ants are throwing a wild rave,
To the rhythm that they crave!

Laughing loudly in leafy nooks,
While squirrels plot with their best hooks.
Under boughs where shadows play,
I'll nap off these silly frays!

Whispering Leaves in Motion

In the breeze, the leaves do sway,
Dancing like a child at play.
A squirrel zooms, then takes a dive,
And laughs at those who just arrive.

The sun peeks through, all aglow,
A cat plays tag, just steals the show.
With every rustle, whispers come,
'You thought you'd nap? Just hear that drum!'

Palm-Sheltered Twilight

Beneath the arching fronds so wide,
A T-Rex toy begins to glide.
He thinks he rules, but what a joke,
As ants march by, they make him choke!

The sun sets slow, a silly dance,
A pair of tourists miss their chance.
They snap a pic, all bugs in view,
With hungry bees that buzzed right through!

Sunlit Avenues of Green

A parrot squawks its loud refrain,
While hippos sip from silver rain.
The path is paved with coconut shells,
Where everyone shares their funny tales.

An old dog snores, a hat on head,
While laughter swirls, our joy widespread.
We all embrace this wacky ride,
With monkey shenanigans on the side!

Hidden Dreams Beneath the Fronds

Under leaves, a toad sings bright,
He croaks his dreams both day and night.
With every jump, he steals the air,
While frogs smile wide without a care.

A hammock hints at lazy fun,
As ants parade like they have won.
Just watch out for the sneaky breeze,
Who plays with hats and brings you knees!

Beneath the Swirling Skies

In a land where coconuts play,
Monkeys steal fruits, what a day!
Sun hats fly in the swirling breeze,
Sunscreen's lost among the trees.

A sunburned dog with shades on tight,
Chases shadows, what a sight!
Tourists laugh, they trip and fall,
As flip-flops fling at a beach ball.

Life's a dance in the sandy spot,
With seagulls plotting a snack plot.
Laughter bounces like bouncing kites,
Underneath all the giggling heights.

Echoes of Tropical Lullabies

Under the moon, a lizard sings,
Croaking tunes of silly things.
Crabs do the cha-cha near the shore,
Who knew crustaceans could dance more?

The stars above blink and sway,
As beach bums snooze the night away.
A fishy friend joins with a splash,
While surfboards take a lazy crash.

Palm fronds wave like hands in cheer,
As night descends, bringing good cheer.
Dreams float on waves, with giggles galore,
Under the moon's silver decor.

Sway and Simmer

Let's get jazzy on the beach,
While sandy toes are within reach.
A parrot chats with a rusty drum,
Stealing laughs with each funny hum.

The sun's a big old fried egg now,
Bathers cramming in, oh wow!
A sunburned crab on sunblock spree,
Tells us the tales from the deep blue sea.

Surfboards stand like they've had a sip,
Of tropical juice on a wobbly trip.
With a splash and a laugh, we play all day,
Embracing summer in a funny way!

Charms of the Coastal Tides

A clamshell holds the secrets still,
But seagulls squawk, they've had their fill.
Fishy jokes fly through salty air,
While mermaids giggle without a care.

Waves come in with a funny crash,
As beach balls roll, what a splash!
Umbrellas dance in a wild breeze,
As wind chimes jingle from palm trees.

Tides whisper secrets to those who listen,
While starfish giggle and glisten.
Oh, this coastline's quite the jest,
With every wave, a funny fest!

Embracing the Horizon's Call

With coconuts falling all around,
I duck and weave without a sound.
A seagull swoops, but too late,
I'm already gone, it's fate!

Flip-flops slapping, what a spree,
They question if I'm really me.
On sand so warm, I do a jig,
While crabs stare back, they sure are big!

Sunbaked laughter fills the air,
As sunscreen battles with my hair.
I seek the waves, they play coy,
Oh beach life, you are my joy!

Then off I go, a snack in hand,
With granola bars, oh isn't it grand?
A seagull swoops for a cheeky bite,
I defend my lunch, ready to fight!

The Path of Celestial Palms

Beneath the leaves, I skip and slide,
Avoiding drips from that tall guide.
My hat takes flight, a bold escape,
While neighbors laugh, what a big gape!

A parrot yells, "Hey, look at that!"
As I lose my balance, give a spat.
I tumble down, a beach-bound clown,
Golden moments turn me upside down!

Flip-flops hang on for dear life,
In this sunlit mishap rife.
I laugh and roll on grains so fine,
In this golden dust, I'm feeling divine!

So onward I go, with sand between toes,
Chasing waves where the sea foam flows.
As giggles carry on the breeze,
I strut to the rhythm of sun-kissed trees!

Murmurs of the Sun-drenched Journey

In the sunlight's warm embrace,
I dance around with style and grace.
A drink spills down my shining chest,
Who knew beach life was such a jest?

A dolphin jumps, "Hello!" it seems,
While I get tangled in my dreams.
I wave back, but lose my hat,
Next thing you know, I'm where it's at!

Round the bend, I spot a kite,
That flies away in a chirpy flight.
My snack takes off, my beachy treat,
Guess I'll just share with the sea, how sweet!

Among the waves, I laugh with glee,
Who knew life had such a spree?
As sunbows dance upon my grin,
I cherish each silly moment within!

Tales from the Shoreline's Embrace

I strolled along where the tides embrace,
My build-a-sandcastle, oh what a place!
It promptly collapsed with just one wave,
But my laughs echoed where dreams behave.

Seagull squawks, then makes a dive,
For my snacks, it's quite the thrive!
I chase it off with flailing arms,
While giggling fills the sandy farms.

With ice cream melting down my hand,
I flip and flop, can't understand.
This sticky life is full of cheer,
As friends shout, "Come join, the coast is clear!"

As sun fades low, with evening's glow,
I find new strength to take it slow.
Amongst the jokes and playful schemes,
I gather moments, weaving dreams!

Golden Arches of Nature

Beneath the sunny rays, we stroll,
With palms that sway, they play a role.
They wave hello, then wave goodbye,
As we walk past, they seem to sigh.

They point the way, with leafy hands,
And laugh at travelers—to their plans.
"Get lost!" they whisper, teasingly,
In this green circus, wild and free.

A parrot jokes, perched high and proud,
While monkeys drop leaves from a cloud.
"Don't mind the mess!" the fruit bats cry,
"Just join our fiesta, oh my, oh my!"

So grab your hats, let's take a chance,
Join the breeze in a silly dance.
At every twist, a giggle or two,
Nature's laughter, all just for you!

Serenity Among the Leaves

In a hush of green, where giggles hide,
Leaves chortle softly, swaying with pride.
A squirrel performs, a nutty ballet,
Nut crunching comedy, brightens the day.

Under the shade, a hammock swings wide,
Catch a quick nap, oh what a ride!
Then a breeze teases, like a playful pup,
"Wake up, sleepyhead! Your coffee's gone up!"

The sunbeams dance through branches so spry,
While critters gossip, "Did you see that guy?"
A turtle in sunglasses, slow as can be,
Turns with a grin, "I'm living carefree!"

So here we gather, with smiles to share,
Among the whispers, we find our flair.
In this leafy realm, laughter takes flight,
With every leaf rustling, the world feels right!

Glistening Canopies

Up above, where the sunlight plays,
Palms wave like flags in the sun's warm rays.
They shimmer and shine with comedic flair,
As squirrels reenact a circus affair.

"Step right up!" they seem to yell,
"See the acrobatics? You'll love them well!"
But one jumps too high, and where does he go?
Land in a palm—a comedic show!

Swinging vines become the stage,
Where laughter bursts, like a turning page.
Frogs join the rhythm with ribbits so loud,
While raccoons clamor, forming a crowd.

So take a stroll, enjoy the sight,
Of nature's jesters, oh what a delight!
In the canvas of green, humor's divine,
Join in the fun, let your spirit shine!

Dancing in the Tropical Breeze

In the balmy air, where hilarity thrives,
Palm fronds are grooving, oh how they jive!
"Come join our party!" they call out to thee,
Under the sway, just dance with glee!

Coconuts chuckle from their lofty tower,
"Watch out below!" they shout with power.
When they take a tumble, what a big splash,
"Look out!" we shout, as we dive in a dash!

The breeze is a DJ, spinning us round,
While flowers toss petals, laughing aloud.
"Keep moving your feet, don't miss the beat,
It's a tropical rave, full of fruity sweet!"

So sway with the palms, kick back, just tease,
In this joyful land, find your inner breeze.
Let every giggle lift you in flight,
In nature's embrace, everything feels right!

Echoes of the Coastal Breezes

Wobbly coconuts take a dive,
Laughter echoes, oh what a vibe.
Sandy toes on a dance floor grand,
Seagulls squawking, unplanned band.

Flip-flops flying, a clumsy whirl,
Sunbathers giggle, hair in a twirl.
Ocean waves play a funky beat,
The beach ball rolls, oh what a treat!

Mischief brewing, a crab joins in,
Snapping claws, a crustacean grin.
Kite surfers zoom above our heads,
Chasing after dreams on their colorful threads.

Breezy whispers, tales of delight,
Coconut drinks, all day and night.
As the sun sets, the stories unfold,
With every laugh, another tale told.

Harvesting Dreams in the Tropics

Planting seeds in sandy beds,
Sunburnt noses and silly threads.
With every sprout, a giggle erupts,
But wait, what's that? A frog in a cup!

Banana peels flying everywhere,
Slip and slide without a care.
The parrots squawk, a raucous choir,
While we sip drinks on a straw-built chair.

Pineapples twirl in a wild dance,
Bouncing around, they take a chance.
Juggling fruit, what a sight to see,
The tropical circus calls out to me!

Under a palm, we scheme and plot,
With dreams as sweet as a toasty hot pot.
Laughing at life, we chase the sun,
Just harvesting joy, and oh what fun!

The Avenue of Singing Palms

Strolling down where the shadows sway,
Palms sing tunes that tickle the day.
A ukulele leaps from a nearby stand,
While the wind hums softly, oh so grand.

Parrots gossip, they're in on the jokes,
Bouncing on branches like cheerful folks.
Swaying to rhythms, a tropical band,
We join the dance, hand in hand.

Flip-flops flapping, a rhythmic beat,
Sandcastles mission—no time for defeat.
A crab on the run, he joins the parade,
As laughter erupts, in sunshine's cascade.

With every step, the palms engage,
Telling stories from a different age.
Finding giggles in the sunlit space,
On this avenue, life's a wild race!

Sunlight Filtering Through the Canopy

Sunbeams wiggle, playful and bold,
Through leafy curtains, stories unfold.
A monkey swings with a cheeky grin,
Chasing the light, let the fun begin!

A picnic basket spills its treasure,
Fruit and sandwiches, simple pleasure.
Ants march in a determined line,
Joining the feast, they think it's fine.

Squirrels chatter, plotting a raid,
While sunflowers stretch, unafraid.
Butterflies flutter, a colorful show,
In this warm hug of a vibrant glow.

Life dances lightly, nothing's amiss,
In a garden of dreams, we find our bliss.
With laughter ringing, let memories grow,
As sunlight filters in, putting on a show.

The Call of Zephyr's Touch

A breeze tickles my nose, so light,
A lizard dances, what a sight!
It leaps with glee, a tiny star,
Chasing shadows from near to far.

Coconuts drop with a plop and a splash,
I dodge and weave, oh what a dash!
An avocado rolls with a thud,
Embracing law of nutty mud.

Swaying palm fronds wave hello,
Each twist and turn puts on a show.
A bird tripped over its own beat,
Guess it was too cool to stay on its feet.

With laughter filling this sunny patch,
Who knew nature knew how to match?
I join the fun, my giggles rise,
Tropical chaos, a grand surprise!

Horizon's Edge of Tropical Whispers

Beneath a sky of candy dreams,
I stroll where sunlight gently beams.
A crab in shades, with style and class,
Declares, 'This beach is my kind of mass!'

Seashells giggle in the sand,
While seagulls make a noisy band.
They steal my fries, with cheeky grace,
My lunch now has a feathered race!

A breeze like laughter, light and free,
Kites flutter joyfully, can't you see?
Fish jump like they've thoughts profound,
Are they planning to dance on ground?

With waves that wink and shout so loud,
I join their fun, I'm feeling proud.
A sunburned nose and wind-tousled hair,
This is living, without a care!

Beneath the Tropical Sky

Here I lie in a hammock swing,
Dreaming of snacks and ice cream 'zing.'
A squirrel swings by, quite the charmer,
With acorns flying, a fuzzy farmer!

Waves crash like a cat's soft paws,
Nature's quirks deserve applause.
Sandcastles lean, a slumping throne,
Royal decrees soon overthrown!

A lizard has on shoes too tight,
Imitating dancers in the light.
A taco truck spins down the lane,
With every twist, I diagnose a gain!

Polls of laughter, the sun goes low,
As evening brings a warm glow.
I sip my drink, watch a bird strut,
Who knew this could be such a riot?

Silhouettes of Tranquility

Under palms, the shadows sway,
I found my hat, oh what a fray!
A monkey on a branch above,
Chased my drink, fell in love!

Footprints lead to joke-filled spots,
Where giggles bubble like lemonade pots.
I'm sailing on flip-flops to laugh,
And dodging crabs with a crafty half!

Sunsets paint the world in gold,
While coconut jokes never grow old.
A pineapple dreams of being a pie,
But insists on being fruity high!

With every wave, a giggle rolls,
And melodies dance in our souls.
Life's a beach, but who would guess,
It's also a stage for pure silliness!

A Breath of Island Air

Breezes dance with haiku grace,
Flip-flops squeak, it's quite a race.
Mango slices, sticky sweet,
Watch out for bees—they're here to greet!

Sunburn stripes, a fashion flair,
Sipping drinks without a care.
Scare a crab, jump back and laugh,
Who knew lunch could run so fast?

Tanned legs high on beachside chairs,
Count the clouds, enjoy the stares.
The seagulls squawk a silly tune,
While we swing like monkeys, whoo-hoo!

Endless giggles, silly sights,
Even dogs wear sun-kissed lights.
Life's a joke—let's have a ball,
With a beach hat that's twice our haul!

The Allure of Green Horizons

Frogs in ties and lizards spin,
Dress code's weird, but who's to win?
Coconuts dodge, a comical fight,
Beneath the palm's umbrella, it's a sight!

Swaying dancers with goofy moves,
In flip-flops, they've got the grooves.
Tropical drinks, umbrellas too,
One sip, and we're flying—who knew?

The monkey jokes, they just won't quit,
Stealing sunglasses—it's quite a hit!
Laughter echoes through the trees,
As nature flirts with fun and breeze.

Shady spots where we all melt,
Giggly snacks from coconut belt.
It's caper time on this green spree,
In a world where laughter's free!

Shimmering Lines of Tranquility

Sunshine drizzles, a zesty splash,
Dining al fresco—a foodie bash.
Salads tumble while we frolic,
We're all wearing colors symbolic!

Laughter bubbles, we make a scene,
With silly hats that smell like green.
Waves that tickle our sandy toes,
The ocean's gossip: who knows?

Kites flying high, we aim to soar,
Giggling kids, we can't ignore.
Dancing shadows beneath the trees,
Even the sun seems to tease.

Cactus jokes and sandy pies,
Mermaids wink, they're sly as spies.
In this canvas of life so bright,
Every giggle a burst of light!

Stories Woven in Green

A hammock sways, it's quite a tease,
With gentle whispers and a warm breeze.
I tell a tale of wild, lost socks,
Adventures grand, like sneaky foxes.

Picnic ants in tiny hats,
They march to join the beachside chats.
Sipping punch (it's got a kick),
While dodging splashes, oh so quick!

The breeze hums songs that itch to dance,
As coconut crabs take their chance.
Every tree a giggle waits,
Each leaf a secret of silly fates.

Our beach tales flow like vivid streams,
In colors bright, and joy's sweet dreams.
Gather 'round, share your fun spin,
In this tapestry where laughs begin!

A Sun-Drenched Boulevard

On a street where sandals squeak,
Sun hats wobble in the heat,
Ice cream drips on eager hands,
Barefoot kids run through the sands.

Sunscreen smears like modern art,
Laughter bursting, a happy heart,
Coconuts roll down the lane,
Someone's lost their shiny brain!

Frisbees fly like birds on high,
Dodging shadows from the sky,
Hats blown off like parachutes,
Rolling laughter, silly hoots.

The path's a loop of joy and fun,
Silly stunts, oh what a run!
A sun-drenched world where quirks abound,
Life's a circus, laughter's found.

Pathways to Paradise Lost

In flip-flops, I took my stride,
With a coconut drink by my side,
Signposts twist in the sandy breeze,
Where'd I leave my car keys, please?

Seagulls squawk like chatty mates,
Dancing crabs with funny gait,
Beach balls bounce, they take a flight,
Underneath the sun so bright.

Maps are lost, oh what a shock,
Can't remember that big rock,
With every turn, a giggle grows,
As I trip on all my woes.

Paths and laughs, they twist and wind,
Paradise? It's hard to find!
But giggles echo in the air,
Who needs a map? Let's just dare!

Leaves of Time

Time flies by like pesky bugs,
Bearing memories, warm as hugs,
Leaves flutter down, they start to dance,
Who knew they'd join this fun romance?

Whispers crackle in the shade,
Silly secrets gently laid,
A squirrel wears a tiny hat,
And points at me with a little spat.

Old jokes linger in the breeze,
Tickled pink by summer trees,
Growth rings laugh, while shadows tease,
How they tease with perfect ease!

Leaves of time in laughter twirl,
Creating chaos in a whirl,
In the branches, giggles rhyme,
Around the world, we laugh at time.

Golden Light Filtering Through

Golden rays play hide and seek,
Through palm fronds, oh so chic,
Caught in laughter, shadows sway,
As giggles light up the day.

Bubbles float like little dreams,
Floating high, or so it seems,
Each one pops with a funny sound,
Echoing joy all around.

In the glow, a dance begins,
With silly twirls and playful spins,
The sunbeams join, a merry crew,
Making faces bright and new.

So take a stroll, let spirits soar,
In this light, who could ask for more?
With laughter sprinkled everywhere,
Joy blooms free in sunny air.

Embraced by the Green Guardians

Beneath the guard of leafy fronds,
Laughter dances with breezy bonds.
A monkey swings, a coconut flies,
'Is that your lunch?' the seagull cries.

What's this strange fruit? Oh, let me guess!
I might just try it, for a fun mess.
With green hats made of nature's style,
Even the tourists pause and smile.

Palm fronds rustle, a gentle sigh,
Whispers of mischief flutter by.
'Watch out for squirrels!' a voice exclaims,
While the local goats play silly games.

A dance-off with crabs, who will win?
Beneath the leaves, the fun begins.
The guardians laugh, they sway and cheer,
In this patch of joy, there's no room for fear.

Melodies of a Coastal Oasis

On sandy shores where laughter rings,
Tide pools shimmer, and seagulls sing.
A crab tap dances, a fish hums low,
While snorkelers giggle at the show.

Waves crash in with a playful splash,
Mermaids giggle, in a bright flash.
A sunburned tourist trips in glee,
He yells, 'I swear that fish winked at me!'

The trees sway to the ocean's beat,
As beach balls soar, and kids run fleet.
Ice cream dribbles down chins so round,
In this silly place, pure joy is found.

So join the fun, don't be shy,
With goofy hats and a sunburned tie.
In this coastal bliss, let laughter reign,
Where every silly moment is our gain.

Silence Among the Leaves

In the shade where silence tends to grow,
A squirrel's chatter is the only show.
Leaves rustle softly with a gentle tease,
'Is that a breeze, or do I hear sneezes?'

A dance of shadows in the afternoon,
Caught in a waltz, a frog croaks a tune.
'Quiet please!' the grasshoppers say,
As a butterfly floats, turning night to day.

Even the whoops of the outlandish birds,
Blend into whispering, silly words.
'Check my moves!' one says with a spin,
Crafting a buzz, trying to win.

In this leafy hush, a giggle breaks free,
An old gnome chuckles, 'Can't catch me!'
For even in silence, joy can be loud,
As laughter erupts, bold and proud.

Armor of Tranquility

A hat of palms, oh what a sight,
Worn by a critter that's quite polite.
Lizards in suits, they strut with flair,
While turtles chuckle without a care.

Beneath the palm's wide leafy shield,
The world outside seems less revealed.
A rendezvous of creatures so bright,
They plan their mischief under hidden light.

Sipping nectar with silly grins,
Hummingbirds argue on who wins.
'Last one to buzz is a lumpy rock!'
And off they zoom, like a comical clock.

In this tranquil scene of merry delight,
Where laughter shields like armor tight.
Nature's jesters in leafy attire,
Craft joy and laughter that'll never tire.

Meditations Under Golden Palms

Underneath the waving leaves,
I found a fried banana thief.
Sipping coconut with glee,
Not sharing, that cheeky bee!

Chilling on a sandy seat,
A crab danced to a silly beat.
He tried to catch a passing wave,
But flipped and flopped, a clumsy rave!

The sunbeams tickle my nose,
While seagulls strike their funny pose.
A parrot squawking oh-so-loud,
I swear he thinks he's in a crowd!

Beneath these golden crowns so bright,
Laughter echoes day and night.
Time drips slowly like sweet jam,
Life's a beach, I'm just a sham!

Sanctuaries of Serenity

In shady spots where laughter lingers,
Turtles wear their sun hats like swingers.
They waddle past with such flair,
I giggle, it's too much to bear!

Breezes tickle through the fronds,
While ants march to their silly songs.
Each step a dance, a tiny jig,
The sun turns all the bugs so big!

With fruit hats piled on my head,
I dance where wise old roots are spread.
Bananas roll and oranges fly,
Nature's circus in the sky!

These moments with my nature pals,
Bring giggles like a thousand calls.
My sanctuary, green and bright,
Where laughter blooms, what a delight!

Currents of the Coastal Breeze

The ocean whispers jokes so smooth,
Crabs try to dance, but they just groove.
A fish flicks water like a spray,
While dolphins leap and shout hooray!

Surfboards slide with comical grace,
As beach balls bounce in every place.
Flip-flops flapping to the beat,
Every stumble's like a treat!

Tanned tourists strike their fanciest pose,
While gulls convene for mischief shows.
They swoop and snatch away my fries,
With cheeky shakes and mischievous eyes!

With giggles tangled in the breeze,
Nature brings us all to our knees.
In this coastal fun and delight,
I'll dance until the sun takes flight!

Nature's Gentle Halls

In tranquil greens where breezes tease,
Butterflies prance with utmost ease.
A busy bee in a buzzing race,
Trips on a petal, what a face!

With rustling leaves above my head,
The squirrels gossip, it's pure bread.
I watch them leap from branch to branch,
With nutty laughs, they twist and prance!

A toad croaks out his own cool song,
While frogs jump in a wild throng.
Each plop is met with hearty cheer,
Nature's laughter loud and clear!

In gentle halls of joy and fun,
Life's a dance, there's always sun.
With every step, I feel so spry,
Nature's laughter, oh my, oh my!

Dreams Under the Sun

Dancing shades of green and brown,
Laughter echoes, bouncing 'round.
Hats so big they fly away,
Sunburnt noses, come what may.

Coconuts fall with a thud,
Sipping drinks, we trudge through mud.
Sandcastles crumble, waves collide,
Chasing crabs, it's quite a ride!

Pathways of Life's Oasis

Flip-flops squeak with every step,
Dodging puddles, one misstep.
Ice cream drips like melting dreams,
Sun more fierce than it truly seems.

Tropical drinks with funny straws,
Getting lost in nature's flaws.
Monkeys chatter with glee and cheer,
We laugh, we slip, we shed a tear.

Tides of Nature's Embrace

Waves like dancers, up and down,
Splashing joy in every town.
Seagulls steal our lunch with flair,
While we balance without a care.

Jellyfish waltz, oh what a show,
Trying to catch a breeze to blow.
Surfboards tumble, shouts and cheers,
Laughter echoes, erasing fears.

The Way to the Tropical Heart

Breezy whispers, secrets shared,
Snorkel gear, oh don't be scared!
Tangled hair from ocean rides,
Chasing sunsets, hearts as guides.

Frisbees flying, laughter loud,
Sunset chasers join the crowd.
Life's a game of hide and seek,
Under palm trees, so unique.

Whispers of the Tropical Breeze

The breeze tickles the leaves, oh so light,
A parrot squawks, causing quite the fright.
Coconuts rolling down with a crash,
I dodge the flying fruits, oh what a splash!

Swaying palms twist in a silly dance,
While monkeys swing about, taking a chance.
They steal my hat, how rude and absurd,
Yet I can't help laughing — they're simply disturbed!

I trip on roots, do a quirky flip,
These trees must conspire, it's a wild trip.
The ground shakes with laughter, can you hear?
Nature's own comedy, oh dear, oh dear!

But who needs a map for this playful spree?
When giggles guide me through every tree.
With each wobbly step, I feel so alive,
In this jungle of joy, I've learned to thrive!

Beneath the Canopy of Green

Under leafy covers, the sun peeks through,
I spot a chameleon — what's it up to?
Changing colors faster than my mind,
It's a fashion show I never designed!

Lizards lounging on a comfy log,
While fluttering butterflies play a game of hog.
They flit and flutter, so silly and free,
Each one a diva but not quite like me!

Beneath the vast expanse of emerald leaves,
I trip over roots, and the tree grieves.
An ant parade marches up my shoe,
I hear them mutter, "What's wrong with you?"

Nature hums tunes that are goofy and bright,
With tunes in the air, I dance with delight.
In the shade of green, I chuckle and sway,
In this silly realm, I'll gladly stay!

Shadows Dance on Sunlit Sand

On golden grains where shadows play,
I watch as sandcastles melt away.
The waves giggle, teasing my toes,
While I try to juggle — hope no one knows!

Seagulls swoop down, all sharp and sly,
Stealing my snacks as they soar by.
They cackle and caw, what a raucous crew,
I'm left with crumbs, oh where's my stew?

A crab with an attitude scuttles in sight,
Waving its claws as if ready to fight.
"Back off!" I yell, but it pinches my toe,
"Why must this beach be such a show?"

Yet amid the chaos and ocean's laugh,
I find a smiling, sandy giraffe.
Together we chuckle at life's silly strand,
In this absurd world, we make our stand!

A Journey Through Leafy Grandeur

In a jungle where giggles echo the most,
I meet a toucan who loves to boast.
With a beak like a banana, big and bright,
It sings off-key, what a hilarious sight!

Beneath towering trees, I trip on a shoe,
Turns out it's a sloth who's stowed it too!
With a yawn and a blink, it slowly grins,
"Why hurry along when joy's where it begins?"

Mosquitoes buzzing like a band gone wrong,
Form a melody, though it's hard to sing along.
I swat and I dance, it's a wild swing,
In this leafy theatre, we all join in!

As I wander through this playful abode,
Each twist and turn just lightens my load.
With laughter as my map, the journey is grand,
In this comedy of leaves, I'm happily banned!

Roots of Resilience

In the sun, they boldly stand,
Roots tangled like a band.
Shouting 'We can take the heat!'
While dodging folks beneath their feet.

Their leaves all dance, quite the show,
Whispering secrets only they know.
A wiggle here, a shimmy there,
Trying hard not to lose a hair!

Oh, the squirrels come, looking sly,
They think they're slick, oh my, oh my!
Planning pranks from their leafy thrones,
While the trunks just moan in low groans.

With laughter ringing through the day,
Even branches join in the play.
These wise old trees sway and spout,
Making every passerby shout out!

Mellowing Palm Shadows

Underneath a leafy shade,
Coconut dreams are quickly made.
Sunbathers nap, sipping sweet drinks,
While palm leaves chatter—what do they think?

The languid breeze brings fuzzy sounds,
As laughter rolls across the grounds.
Watch out, a rogue piña colada flies!
Better duck, or get a sweet surprise!

The shadows grow stretch like a cat,
Enticing folks to sit and chat.
'You look hot!' laughs one nearby,
Under these leaves that wave like a guy.

But oh, beware the sticky feet,
From spilled treats now made complete.
Mellowing shadows hug the ground,
In this paradise, how fun is found!

Rhythm of Swaying Palms

With every gust, they wiggle and sway,
In their little dance, come join the fray.
Twisting and turning, they boast and brag,
'We're the coolest trees in the whole bag!'

Ukuleles strum, seagulls squawk,
As palm fronds tap in a rhythmic talk.
Shadows shaking, they're hip to the beat,
Creating a floor for loosening feet!

Two squirrels spin in a dizzy duet,
Chasing each other without a fret.
They tangle in leaves—oh, what a sight!
Nature's own show, pure delight!

So if you hear that rustling cheer,
Know it's the palms calling you near.
Softly they sway, with giggles abound,
In their vibrant world, joy is found!

Echoes of Coastal Dreams

In the distance, laughter rings,
As the wind flirts, and the coastline sings.
Palm trees lean in a cool embrace,
Whispering secrets of this vibrant place.

'What do you know?' asks a nearby frond,
'Oh please, tell me, respond!'
They tickle the sky with a cheeky smile,
As tourists pause and laugh awhile.

Seashells scatter, glistening bright,
Under the palm trees, pure delight.
Kids building castles, feeling so free,
While palm leaves shimmy like they're on spree.

And when the sun sets, an orange hue,
The palms just chuckle, 'Look at that view!'
Echoes of joy, dancing through night,
When palms dream up their next delight!

Secrets of the Swaying Branches

In the breeze they dance and twirl,
With fronds that tease and unfurl.
A coconut on head, oh dear!
Watch your step, or a snack is near!

They whisper tales of sunny days,
And laugh at ants in their silly ways.
With every sway, a secret shared,
Bizarre antics I never dared!

A monkey swings with style and grace,
While pigeons strut, a feathery race.
The branches bend and creak with cheer,
As if they know we're gathered here!

A party blooms beneath their shade,
With laughter, snacks, and games well played.
Oh, who knew trees could bring such glee?
They're the life of this leafy spree!

Heartbeat of the Tropics

With roots in mud and dreams on high,
The leafy lords reach for the sky.
They tickle clouds in playful jest,
While critters scurry, never rest.

Each swing and sway is like a dance,
Creating laughter, taking a chance.
With every twist, a chuckle found,
As branches hug the merry ground.

The sun peeks through, a playful tease,
The shadows flicker, sway with ease.
What tricks will two bugs try today?
Can they outsmart that cheeky jay?

In the heart of this leafy thrum,
Life's vibrant stories never humdrum.
Nature's jesters, so full of cheer,
Tickling our hearts when they appear!

Underneath the Verdant Boughs

We gather 'neath the verdant crowd,
Where laughter bursts and spirits loud.
Blades of grass tickle toes,
While nature's humor surely grows!

A leaf drops down, a leafy dare,
Swiping hats from heads laid bare.
The sun can't help but crack a grin,
As breezes spin the spinny kin.

A squirrel juggles, oh what a sight!
Three acorns tumbling left and right.
With every slip, a giggle flies,
As nature's pranks light up the skies.

Oh, what joy beneath this green dome,
A wild haven that feels like home.
A festival of fun, we replay,
Underneath the boughs, we laugh and play!

A Passage Through Gentle Giants

In a forest where the giants grow,
They sway and giggle, don't you know?
With each creak, they share a joke,
While passing clouds around them poke.

A bird takes aim at a wandering hat,
Hovering easy, then a swift spat.
The trees all chuckle at the new game,
As the hat flies high, winging through fame.

They whisper secrets, stories wide,
Of wandering folks who giggle and glide.
Through branches thick, we wander free,
With every step, a legacy.

So dance, oh giants, sway with grace,
In this wild and hallowed space.
Together we'll laugh, together we'll sway,
In this passage of joy, forever we'll play!

Heartstrings of Nature's Wonder

In the breeze, a leaf falls down,
It tickles my nose, oh what a clown!
A squirrel leaps high, a cheeky chap,
With acorns as snacks, he plans his nap.

Birds in a chorus, a silly tune,
They dance on branches, under the moon.
A frog in a hat sings loud, oh dear,
I can't help but laugh, it's a riot here!

The sun winks down from skies so blue,
As bugs in tuxedos give a debut.
Nature's stage, oh what a sight,
With giggles and grace, it feels just right.

So skip with joy, let out a cheer,
In this wild show, there's nothing to fear.
With whimsy and wonder, let's all partake,
In this nature's jest, for giggles' sake!

A Dance of Leaves and Light

Leaves twirl about in a joyful spree,
An impromptu dance, just for me!
A butterfly pirouettes with flair,
As laughter bounces in the warm air.

The sun plays peek-a-boo with a grin,
While a worm in a top hat walks with kin.
They wiggle and giggle, a funny sight,
In the glimmering glow of soft daylight.

A caterpillar busts a move so smooth,
While ants in a line are trying to groove.
With every twist and every sway,
Nature's folly leads the way!

They shimmied and they jived, a leafy mess,
As I joined in, wearing my best dress.
With heartbeats echoing a silly tune,
Let's dance together 'neath the bright moon!

Dreams Beneath Verdant Skies

Clouds wear hats that are fluffy and grand,
While daisies tickle at my hand.
A rabbit pops in for a quick chat,
Says, "Why wear shoes? Just chill with that!"

Kites in the sky are laughing away,
On gusty breezes, they frolic and play.
A dragonfly dressed as a tiny ace,
Whirls around with such style and grace.

Beneath green canopies, shadows prance,
While worms on the ground do a little dance.
Life is a show, oh what a scene,
With giggles and joy, bright and serene.

So close your eyes and dream real sweet,
Where nature's humor can't be beat.
In bushy fields, where laughter blends,
These verdant dreams are where it all ends!

The Way of Nature's Whisper

Whispers of grass tickle my toes,
As ants with swagger strike silly poses.
A cloud lets out a loud, silly sigh,
While giggling streams flow softly by.

Branches wave like they're in a race,
Tickling one another in a green embrace.
A chattering bird sings off-key,
In its own world, just being free!

Frogs in a chorus, don't miss a beat,
With jazz hands out, they can't be beat.
The daisies chuckle, bending with glee,
In nature's sitcom, there's always a spree.

So join this ride, where laughter's a tune,
Beneath a bright and giggly moon.
With nature's voice, come dance and sway,
And let your worries just float away!

Shadows of Sunlit Shores

On sandy strips where shadows play,
A crab with shades attempts to sway.
He sidesteps quick, a funny dance,
In hopes to catch a seagull's glance.

With UV rays that burn quite bright,
A sunburned tourist takes flight.
He leaps and yells, sweater in tow,
While sun hats tumble in the flow.

A coconut falls, quite the surprise,
It bounces off a guy's sun-kissed thighs.
He shrieks and jumps, a wild display,
As beachgoers chuckle at his ballet.

The ocean laughs, it sweeps and pulls,
As surfboards wobble, causing spills.
Umbrella hats fly, the scene steals time,
In this comical, sunny clime.

Breeze-Kissed Tropics

Amidst the palms, a parrot squawks,
Stealing snacks, and making mocks.
A tourist fumbles with his drink,
It splashes out! What's in the pink?

A hammock swings as laughter soars,
While sleepyheads dream of surfboard scores.
One snores aloud, a dreadful tune,
The other spins like a balloon.

A beach ball flies like it's possessed,
Knocks over sunbathers—what a mess!
They shout and yell, "Not my tan!"
While others giggle at the grand plan.

Through coconut groves and laughter close,
A chap trips over his own toes.
In breezy bliss, mischief does thrive,
In these tropics, we come alive!

Traces of Paradise

Footprints lead to a jellyfish show,
A child leaps back, yells "Oh no!"
With wiggly tails that dance on sand,
He runs so fast, who would've planned?

A sunhat flies far from its throne,
As seagulls squawk with voices prone.
They dive and swoop, want a bite,
But all they find is pure delight.

Ice cream melts, drips down a cone,
While flavors mix; what's this? A groan!
A sticky hand now grabbing more,
A beach bum's dream, can't ignore.

In these traces of blissful days,
We laugh and chortle in goofy ways.
Life rolls like waves, in vibrant cheer,
As chuckles echo far and near.

Treetop Serenade

The leaves above start rustling tunes,
As monkeys swing with cheeky swoons.
They toss coconuts like they're gold,
While perplexed tourists just fold.

A parrot sings off-key, so loud,
Interrupts the sun, draws a crowd.
With every squawk, a giggle flows,
As folks are served by nature's prose.

A swing between two palm trees swings,
And someone's trapped with silly strings.
Lost in laughter, stuck in play,
A true vacation in shades of gray.

In treetop heights, where fun takes flight,
We find our joy, a pure delight.
With every jest and giggle shared,
In this serene world, we've dared.

Celestial Gardens of the Coast

In fields where coconuts roll,
A crab plays the bongo with soul.
The seagulls dance with flair,
While flip-flops float through the air.

With piña colada in hand,
My dance moves are totally unplanned.
A toucan laughs from a tree,
As I trip on a root—oh, woe is me!

The sunsets spill paint on the shore,
While I search for my towel once more.
I thought it was pink, but it's blue,
Guess it's koala in color, who knew?

So here's to the chaos and cheer,
Where jellyfish give us a sneer.
We waddle like ducks, and it feels so right,
In gardens where laughter takes flight!

Beneath the Tropical Stars

Under stars that giggle and blink,
I sip from a coconut and think.
Did a monkey steal my flip-flop?
Or was it the mermaid who ordered a mop?

The night plays tricks with its light,
As I dance with crabs, oh what a sight!
Bamboo canes sway, laughing low,
As I attempt the limbo…oh no, oh no!

A hammock calls, but I see a bear,
Oh wait, it's just a guy with no hair.
He juggles coconuts and fish,
With dreams of being a tropical dish!

So under these tropical stars,
With laughter and hope, we raise our jars.
Let's stumble and giggle till dawn's light,
For this silly night feels just right!

Lush Lanes of Comfort

In lanes where the lizards do race,
And sunhats are worn with such grace.
I trip on a pineapple slice,
And shout 'this isn't very nice!'

The breadfruit rolls down the street,
While children chase it with bare feet.
A monkey steals my ice cream cone,
And winks like it's all in good tone.

Beneath each leaf, giggles collide,
As I search for my pride and my stride.
Lush lanes twist and spin like a game,
With laughter that shines like a flame.

So here's to the mishaps and glee,
Where life is as wacky as can be!
I'll sip on my drink and embrace the fun,
In these lanes where comfort has won!

Journey Through Whispering Isles

Through isles where palm fronds whisper,
I chase a toucan, my giggling sister.
She says to blend in, 'be like a tree!'
But I'm more of a tumbleweed, you see!

The waves crash like laughter on rocks,
While fruits wear sunglasses like clocks.
"Time to chill!" says a passing whale,
As I wave back, tails in a flail.

We spot a crab with a hat so grand,
He tips it low, what a classy brand!
He moonlights as a dance-floor king,
While I just let loose and swing!

So here's to the journey, the tales unfold,
In isles where silliness strikes gold.
With laughter and joy, let's roam and play,
For this magical trip is here to stay!

Island Secrets in the Wind

In a land where coconuts dance,
Laughter echoes, a silly romance.
Seagulls gossip, with beaks all aglow,
Whoever thought crabs could be so slow!

Sunburnt tourists in sun hats too wide,
Chasing the waves, this is quite the ride.
Flip-flops flying, a comedic sight,
While rogue beach balls take flight in delight.

Sandcastles teeter, then suddenly fall,
Children giggle, they're having a ball.
Mermaids whisper beneath the warm tide,
Sharing their secrets, they chuckle with pride.

Tiki drinks in hand, let's find a good spot,
With umbrellas waving, who needs a whole lot?
A symphony of fun, laughter so sweet,
Island secrets hidden beneath our bare feet.

A Tapestry of Green

Lush leaves tangle, a confused embrace,
Chameleons wiggle, lost in the race.
Vines twist and twirl in a comical show,
While toucans question, 'What's this, though?'

Frogs in tuxedos plan with such flair,
Hopping to meetings, they have much to share.
Kidding around, they launch a grand play,
Who knew jungle life could be this way?

In the thickets, laughter meets the breeze,
An iguana smirks, 'Look, I'm just so pleased!'
With a flick of his tail, he models with grace,
Even the raccoons join in the chase.

Leaves rustle with giggles, the trees join the fun,
As squirrels debate who's the fastest one.
A tapestry woven with smiles and light,
In this jungle of joy, everything feels right.

Nature's Graceful Icons

Behold the flamingo, standing on one,
Its pose a masterpiece, oh what fun!
Balance is key, they flaunt with a wink,
While nearby hippos suddenly rethink.

Turtles in shades, lounging with style,
Move at a speed that can take a while.
Yet, when a picnic begins to ignite,
They're on a mission, a snack snatch delight.

Parrots recounting tales bold and brash,
Their feathers loud, making quite the splash.
With a cheeky grin, they mimick our chat,
Causing great laughter, imagine all that!

Nature's icons prance, with pizzazz in their stride,
Creating a vibe where wonders collide.
Here, comedy blooms amidst splashes of hue,
A joyous crescendo with each passing view.

Pathway of the Tropical Breeze

Along the shore, where palm fronds sway,
Sandy feet shuffle, oh let's dance away!
A crab in a tux, he struts with such pride,
While jellyfish giggle, in the tide they glide.

Waves making music, a rhythm divine,
A rhythm so silly, caught up in the line.
Beach balls bounce crazily, round and round,
As laughter erupts, pure joy can be found.

Sunsets like paintings, colors so bright,
As fireflies gather, they twinkle with light.
Join the parade, don your wildest hat,
Each step brings laughter, can you believe that?

So stroll down this path where folly does reign,
With smiles as treasures, let's dance in the rain.
A pathway of mirth where the breezes tease,
Together we'll wander with playful ease.

www.ingramcontent.com/pod-product-compliance
Lightning Source LLC
Chambersburg PA
CBHW072121070526
44585CB00016B/1521